SECRET GARDENS

OF NEWPORT RHODE ISLAND'S HISTORIC POINT SECTION

Photography by Laurie E. Sullivan

Text by Thomas Gannon

BENEFACTORS OF THE ARTS, LTD.

NEWPORT, RHODE ISLAND

THE SECRET GARDEN TOUR

On the tenth anniversary of the Secret Garden Tour I am pleased to introduce this book of our Secret Gardens. Thanks to our volunteers and gardeners of the past nine years we have been privileged to show the school children of Aquidneck Island the wonders of the Arts, concerts in the school, plays written and developed by the students, computer keyboards that make the music come alive. Dozens of programs that may have helped children to become aware of a world they might otherwise not have known.

It is a wonderful experience to combine the sharing of these beautiful gardens with the sharing of the Arts with the school children. Everybody wins with this program, be it the child hearing "Peter and the Wolf" for the first time or the gardening enthusiast who has never had the pleasure of touring Newport's very special Point Section. This book turns a day full of memories into a tangible creation, to be shared and enjoyed for years to come. This book also will help us continue to do the very important job of spreading the word about the wonders of the Arts to many more deserving children. My thanks goes out to everyone who has helped make Newport's Secret Garden Tour such a success, and to all of those who will help us in the future. —Myra H. DuVally, *President, Benefactor of the Arts*

BOOK DESIGN: DARCY MAGRATTEN, ILLUSTRATIONS: MARIAN L. O'CONNELL, MADELINE R. PORTER, DARCY MAGRATTEN
ADVISORS: MYRA H. DUVALLY, DOUGLAS PENN STICKLEY, THOMAS HASLAM, TONY D. BESSINGER

The Historic Point

Gardens and gardening have been a passion for Point residents, and many Newporters, since the early 1700s. As a leading seaport of the time, Newport was exposed to foreign cosmopolitan influences and developed a wealthy merchant class, whose members could afford fine homes and well-kept grounds. The Point, which lay north of the city center and the main harbor, began developing as a neighborhood after 1725, when a prominent Quaker family, the Eastons, bought up much of the area and began selling lots. Shipwright Street, now Bridge Street, was the first to be occupied, by the craftsmen who attended the ships and the captains who commanded them. Water Street, renamed Washington Street after the Revolution, soon became the site for a row of prosperous merchants' houses, whose front yards overlooked the inner harbor and a succession of private docks.

Newport traders brought back exotic plants and trees from various ports of call, and a town garden might contain such specimens as orange, lemon, and tamarind trees, not all of which took in the Newport climate. The fondness for trees, however, is evident on the Point to this day: To the north of Bridge Street, all the cross streets are named for them—Poplar, Walnut, Willow, and so on. These early gardens tended to be formal after the European tradition and often were truly secret gardens, hidden behind high brick walls and locked iron gates.

Although the Point, with the rest of the city, suffered through three years of occupation by British troops during the Revolution, and later from the inevitable decline of the sea trade, it retains more than one hundred of its early dwellings. And among the inhabitants there is still a penchant for planting decorative gardens. With few exceptions, these gardens are more modest in scale and design, sized to fit city lots that shrank as the neighborhood rebuilt. But they still contain unexpected species, a legacy of their forebears (local lore holds that the rosa rugosa, so suited to the Point's seaside climate, arrived as seeds in the dirt ballast of China Traders). While many are hidden from view like the earlier walled gardens, their generous owners share them with the public once each year during the Secret Gardens Tour.

88 WASHINGTON STREET

There is a lot going on in Anne Reynolds' salt air garden overlooking Narragansett Bay. In June, spiky pink Veronica balances yellow tickweed, while purple geranium blooms against a background of rosy red centranthus. Open to wind and weather and only partially protected by a garden shed—the deck cabins from an old Fall River steamship—the garden demands hardy plants and constant experimentation. "My point is to get drifts of things that people can see and enjoy. I have to try a lot of things just to see what grows," Reynolds says. She has planted a second garden, inside the front gate, a shady spot filled with pink and white astilbe and yellow oenothera. This is for the enjoyment of passersby, who often pause to admire the decorative beehive oven done in clam shells on the exterior of this tiny 1720s cottage, moved here to its seaside site from Providence.

Campanula glomerata
Centranthus ruber
Oenothera
Coreopsis (Tickseed)
Aster xfrikartii
Geranium sanguineum

57 SECOND STREET

*A*n enclosed slate courtyard with statuary stationed here and there gives this garden, Joseph Vars says visitors tell him, "an Italianate feel." One of the more interesting pieces is a three-tiered fountain, topped by an early nineteenth-century lion's head, which was salvaged from a demolished building in Boston. A florist by profession, Vars is sparing in the use of color and plantings in his own back yard. "It's not overgrown," he says. Ivy vines, wood ferns, and an oval of grass in the center make for lots of green. There is color as well. Lily of the valley, azalea, and lilac grow in border beds. Wood violets and white alyssum, their seeds kept warm by the slate, bloom each year between the cracks of the stones. "My annuals are perennials," Vars says.

Azalea

Alyssum

Viola (Violet)

Woodsia (Wood fern)

Convallaria majalis
   (Lily of the Valley)

18 SECOND STREET

Impatiens
Clematis
Rhododendron
Geranium

here is little wonder that this busy garden has been nicknamed the "Jungle Garden" by visitors awed by the dense and varied foliage introduced, says Maurice de La Valette, "as God or nature would have planned, rather than a garden designer." Flowering dogwoods, tree trunk poles supporting an arbor, white-bloom roses reaching up 20 feet, and climbing clematis vines contribute to the tropical feel. The "undergrowth" consists of pink and white impatiens, rhododendrons, and other annuals and perennials. Berry bushes provide fruit for the family into the fall. A pied wooden cow, wood tulips, ceramic cats, and other ornaments supplement nature. "This is a space that my wife Lynn and I enjoy," de La Valette says. "I want to be living here on the Point and feel I'm in the country."

43 WASHINGTON STREET

A semi-formal English cutting garden behind the Greek Revival house at 43 Washington Street produces perfume for the air as well as flowers for the table. The centerpiece of this carefully designed garden is a diamond pattern around a birdbath. A hedge of fragrant lavender outlines the diamond, which is anchored by four boxwood shrubs. Inside, cranberry cotoneaster and euonymus, two natives of Asia, act as ground cover. Outside, boxwood hedges contain peonies, lilies, roses, and irises. The back border is formed by towering arborvitae shrubs and fragrant Japanese lilac. "Flowers are all that we wanted, just nice flowers," says Suzette Seigel. A slate walkway leads one through the garden and to a bench at the far end. But the garden can be enjoyed from several vantage points—from the adjoining brick patio, from the back porch, and from the kitchen window.

Euonymus

Syringa (Japanese Lilac)

Buxus (Boxwood)

Arborvitae

Cotoneaster apiculatus
   (Cranberry Cotoneaster)

36 WALNUT STREET

Alcea (Hollyhock)
Kalmia latifolia (Mountain Laurel)
Clematis
Columbine

*R*estraint and attention to scale keep this private courtyard garden in proportion and pleasing to the eye. When Henry and Suzanne Foster moved into their compact red 1740 colonial house (known to neighbors as the "Pineapple House"), they also took on the task of "bringing back a neglected garden" by raising its level, rebricking the yard, and installing drains. Instead of a profusion of flowers, which might overwhelm this 20' x 25' space, plantings are carefully grouped, each with a purpose. Holly, yew, and lilac hedge surround an herb garden with a fountain as its centerpiece. A small cutting garden contains lots of color—pink mountain laurel, columbine, and hollyhock. Day lilies and coral-bells break up green borders. The overall effect is one of shade, seclusion, and cool retreat.

Phlox

Platycodon (Balloon Flower)

Coreopsis

Huechera sanguinea (Coral-bell)

Stewartia pseudocamellia
  (Japanese Stewartia)

Leucothoe catesbaei
  (Drooping Leucothoe)

57 THAMES STREET

This is a large, open garden with many points of interest. Janet Kasperson says her garden "just evolved" over the years, with borders developing into flower beds and new areas blossoming as a shrub or tree was planted. Two large maples provide shade at the north and south ends of the yard; the rest is sunny. The main flower bed along the western side contains "a hodge-podge" of lily, iris, and other perennials. A smaller bed nearby, marked with a miniature spruce, offers red phlox, pink coreopsis, and astilbe. Around the south corner of the house, Paul Kasperson has created a shaded rock garden, with a variety of hoyas, more astilbe, and European wild ginger. What's next? Maybe a water garden, Kasperson says. Like the proverbial river, one doesn't get to stand in the same garden twice.

29 SECOND STREET

The backyard garden at 29 Second Street has many aspects, all of them casual and friendly. Instead of being arranged in formal beds, the more than 115 varieties of flowers and shrubs are grouped informally. "We wanted it to look like it was unplanned, as though it just happened," says Sue Bowen. "People like it because it's manageable." From the back deck, the eye travels naturally to a cluster of bellflower, bee balm, and spiky Dianthus barbatus. Deeper into the garden, a granite love seat overlooks a water garden, populated by meandering koi fish and surrounded by nelumbo, nymphaea, and other aquatic plants. Here and there, the air carries the scent of rosemary and oregano. The weigela shrub in the far southeast corner catches the last sun of the day and provides a favorite late-afternoon reading spot.

Nymphaea
Monarda (Bee balm)
Campanula (Bellflower)
Rosa Floribunda
Oxalis adenophylla (Chilean Oxalis)
Palaver nudicaule (Iceland Poppy)

54 Washington Street/Hunter House
Preservation Society of Newport County

*T*he formal garden at Hunter House, with its neat boxwood hedges and balanced flower beds, technically is closer to Federal than to Colonial period in design. Nevertheless, it is an apt reflection and fitting complement to the elegant symmetry of this 1748 home, considered by architectural historians to be one of the finest examples of mid-eighteenth century domestic architecture in existence. "The design is actually a nineteenth century design—American post-Colonial," says T. Plimpton, who, with his wife, Susie, conceived the landscaping in 1988. And although "not really a restoration," Plimpton says, the designers did attempt to remain faithful to both the period and Hunter House's particular history. William Hunter, who bought the house in 1805, was a lawyer and politician, whose improvements to the grounds included the planting of berry and rose bushes, quince trees, and grape vines over an arbor.

Delphinium
Aster
Paeonia
Malus floribunda (Crab Apple)
Malus hupehensis (Tea Crab)
Rosa Rugosa

"The garden was designed to represent things that could have been in a typical garden of the time," Plimpton says, although on a grander scale because of its public nature. Two lines of crab apple trees (three tea crabs to the south, four floribunda crabs on the north) are a tribute to Ambassador Hunter's fruit trees. Two trellises, now covered with wisteria, provide shade and an echo of the earlier arbor. On the water side, near the gate to what once was the front yard of the house, is an herb garden, obligatory for any kitchen garden of the period. The main flower garden, with its asters, peonies, and delphiniums, is a study in blues, yellows, and pinks– "soft colors, because the older plants tended to be pastels."

*T*he Sweet Bay magnolia tree by the front gate is the only hint of the hidden garden tucked behind this 1840s dwelling. "It's an American cottage garden, very enclosed and private," says Loretta Goldrick. A border of deep green Baltic ivy, dotted with tulips in spring and Coral-bells in summer, runs the length of the yard from the gate. To the back is a raised perennial garden, rich with creams and yellows—digitalis, rudbeckia, and lamb's-ears. On either side are honey locust trees, "to give the garden height," Goldrick says. Other specimens include a June-flowering Kousa dogwood, a Chinese witch-hazel tree, and a parrotia, all courtesy of horticulturist and arborist Ralph Sabetta, who designed the garden. Along the northern edge of the garden are three varieties of clematis vines, which flower in turn through three seasons. Also to the north, within sight and scent of the patio, is a bed of English Heritage roses behind a border of fragrant lilac.

Rudbeckia

Digitalis (Foxglove)

Clethra

Stachys (Lamb's-ears)

Clematis jackmanii

Acer pseudoplatanus
   (Sycamore Maple)

57 FAREWELL STREET

*A*trip to the Orient inspired the Japanese-style garden in the large back yard of this double Colonial house on the outskirts of the Point. Considering the city's extensive China trade activity and the role of native son Matthew Perry in opening Japan to trade in 1853, an oriental garden "seemed appropriate to an eighteenth-century house in Newport," says Mary Riggs. Japanese elements include the flowing lines of the garden, the extensive use of evergreens, and the peaceful sounds of water splashing in several copper lily pad fountains. Although a Kousa dogwood and a Japanese cherry tree offer delicate blooms, the garden remains green most of the year, with hostas, European wild ginger, Japanese painted fern, and stephanandra ground cover. "You get the feeling of serenity from having these plant materials, instead of the jubilation of flowers," Riggs says.

Asarum (Wild Ginger)
Athyrium goeringianum (Painted Fern)
Enkianthus campanulatus (Redvein Heath)
Stephanandra

101 WASHINGTON STREET

*A*rtist and writer Anita McAndrews has turned her side yard into "kind of an English garden, with lots of flowers for cuttings for the house." There is an air of informal order about her garden. A circular rose garden surrounds a dolphin fountain brought from Italy by a family friend. A bricked area, planted by an earlier owner, is the "Biblical garden," containing only plants cited in the Bible. Among them are Lady's Mantle and Rose of Sharon. Beside another fountain, bright perennials bloom all spring and summer—pink Sweet William, yellow oenothera, purple campanula. About the grounds there are sculptures, including a Labrador dog by Ted Grosvenor, Anita's father. "It's informal," McAndrews says. "The grandchildren come and they love it."

Alchemilla

Astilbe

Dianthus barbatus
   (Sweet William)

Hibiscus syriacus
   (Rose of Sharon)

Hosta
Aquilegia (Columbine)
Azalea
Lonicera (Honeysuckle)
Crocus
Rhododendron

58 THAMES STREET

This is a green garden for much of the year. Given a shady spot with just a smattering of early morning and high noon sun, Bobbi Wright has given up the attempt to grow roses and instead has filled her yard with many types of hostas, lilies (a cousin), columbine, and other low-sunlight varieties. "It's a shade garden," Wright says. "We try to keep everything moist and green." Evergreen shrubs and herbaceous plants over a pachysandra ground cover create cool "wooded areas" along the borders, where maple and cedar trees provide shade. For variation, there is an annuals cutting garden at the rear of the house and ranks of white, pink, and pinker still impatiens, creating "swoops of color," Wright says. In the spring, first color comes with the flowering of crocuses and columbine.

29 ELM STREET

*I*lse Nesbitt has taken advantage of every corner of this courtyard garden in an ell behind Third & Elm Press. Dwarf peach, plum, and apple trees and blueberry and raspberry bushes line the north end. A topiary rooster clipped from yew stands amid the kitchen herb garden. Arborvitae, Rose of Sharon, and early-flowering lilac form the back border to the east, above a bed of pink and yellow perennials—zinnia, dahlia, and Klondike cosmos. Nesbitt was born in Germany and spent her early years in Japan. "Both countries are crowded, so they tend to think in terms of small spaces," she says. A bricked corner, slowly giving way as the garden expands, serves as an extra room in the summer for Nesbitt, husband Alexander, and the family cats. "Every inch is full," she says of the garden that she began in 1966. "It all grows in one happy jamboree."

Zinnia
Alyssum
Klondike Cosmos
Gerbera

Clematis

Viburnum

Achillea

Sedum

Hedera helix (English Ivy)

Wisteria sinensis

20 WILLOW STREET

*P*amela Kelley's L-shaped garden is one of the larger and sunnier plots on the Point, with lots of lawn and a few colorful focal points. At one end, a loose grouping of alchemilla, achillea, sedum, and ornamental grass surrounds a brick patio and fountain. Against the fence (low enough to peer over), an ornamental bench is framed by wisteria. "I try to create interest without closing things down," Kelley says. "I like the sun and the open space." Much of the activity takes place along the borders—a dogwood tree in one corner, a white hydrangea in another spot, purple and white flowering clematis reaching over the front fence. Behind the house, where a red brick patio is much used in warmer months, a curving row of Ilex and a sprinkling of begonia forms the border. Here, Kelley says, "I try to keep it looking mono-chrome—green and some white accents."

3 BRIDGE STREET

Hyacinthus
Paeonia (Peony)
Hemerocallis (Day Lily)

Red brick walkways, spaced cypress trees, and clipped boxwood hedges are orderly elements that suit the adjoining house, a tidy 1750 colonial with finely graduated clapboards. But all is not symmetry in this garden, begun in the early 1970s. "We wanted to have lots of flowers blooming all the time," says James Michael, so the beds were planted almost to overflowing with perennials that blossom in succession throughout the season. Peonies, hyacinths, and daffodils all compete for the sun. "Inside the formal element, the planting is informal," says Richard Nelson. The logic takes into account the wisteria-covered ruins of a 1919 terra cotta outbuilding, an early paint and wallpaper shop, that dominates the north end. "It is a very romantic look, and we like that," Nelson says.

53 WASHINGTON STREET

*W*ith a three-story colonial house set high upon a Victorian era foundation, master gardener Toni Peters wanted a garden that emphasized the vertical. The most striking element is the Belgian terrace that creates a wall defining the back border of the yard. This is an espaliered line of seventeen alternating apple and pear trees, eight feet high, bows entwined in intricate fan and palmette patterns—a 1300s design favored by George Washington at Mount Vernon. To one side, a pergola serves as host for a trumpet vine. By the front gate, a linden tree and an antique Stayman apple tree continue the theme. "I believe in creating rooms when you have a small lot," says Peters. "The front yard is a room, the back yard is a room." Peters prefers flowering shrubs to flowers. The overall effect is a soothing green, but the campsis vine blooms a bright gold in later summer, the fruit trees first thing every spring.

Campsis

Spiraea

Chrysanthemum xsuperbum (Shasta Daisy)

Pyrus Atlantic Queen

77 Bridge Street

Iris danfordiae

Iris pseudacorus

Galanthus (Snowdrop)

Cornus sericea (Red Twig Dogwood)

There may be other species of flowers and flowering shrubs in Herb Rommel's three-lot garden, but irises—dozens of varieties, hundreds of plants—are the main event here, from April through June. Capt. Rommel began collecting iris plants while in the Navy and started his garden on the Point after he retired in 1969. Irises surround the house, dot the lawn under apple trees, and fill out a private garden, hidden behind an old shed. "They're easy to grow, especially the beardless ones," he says. "And they give me a show." Irises are prized for their range of colors, from pure white to creamy lemon to lavender to deep, almost black, purple. His wife, Mary, prefers pink; but the Rommel garden covers the spectrum—white Admiral Nimitz, yellow Danford, rusty Fiesta Sun, and Grapesickle, one of the purple varieties that seem to dominate the genus. But, says Rommel, "You can have a wonderful iris garden without any purples."

8 WILLOW STREET

There are no willows to be found at The Willows, Pattie Murphy's house (it is named after the street); but there is much else to engage both eye and nose. "My idea of a garden is that it's meant to touch a number of the senses," Murphy says. For color, she has pink and white spiderflowers in a clematis-shrouded courtyard, pompon-like allium, and blue and white hydrangea bushes in the main garden. Murphy has used shrubs and flower beds to create a series of outdoor "rooms" in the lighter colors she prefers—white, pink, and blue—to give visitors the illusion of being alone in the garden. For fragrance, she has planted pink English roses and Oriental lilies. "I also want life in the garden," she says, so she has distributed buddleia shrubs and bird feeders about the yard as an invitation to passing butterflies and birds.

Allium
Buddleia (Butterfly Bush)
Cleome (Spiderflower)
Geranium
Hydrangea quercifolia (Oak-leaved Hydrangea)

Notes

This book is dedicated to the gardeners of the Point past, present, and future.

Thank you.